Searching for the Truth

Poems & Prose Inspired by Our Inner Worlds

Written By: Maranda Russell

Copyright 2013 Maranda Russell
All Rights Reserved

For everyone who isn't afraid to search for the truth, even if it means looking outside your comfort zone.

Introduction

This book has been niggling at the back of my mind for years. I have always been interested in the inner worlds - that which goes on in our hearts, minds and souls. I have spent much of my life searching for what I thought was the "truth", only to find that the world of thought is not as black and white as it may seem. There are many questions, many mysteries that may never be sufficiently answered on this side of life, but perhaps that is the way it is supposed to be. In order to continually grow, we need to always be learning and discovering new ideas.

I am happy to say that I have found a sense of inner peace and meaning from all my searching, but I never want to pretend like I know it all. In fact, when I come across people who are sure they know "the truth" entirely, I generally distrust their claims. For that reason, I want to make it clear that the writings in this book are only expressions of my own search for truth and meaning. In no way are these meant to be taken as fact. It is fine if you disagree with my beliefs and thoughts. Sometimes I disagree with myself. There is still much I have to learn and I am comfortable knowing that.

As you read through the poems and prose in this book, know that much of what I'm sharing is deeply personal. Some of the writings here are passages taken straight out of my journals and personal blog posts. At times the things I write may seem to contradict one another, but I am the kind of person who likes to try and see things from both sides if I can. You will find a wide range of subjects covered since many things fall into the realm of the inner life.

You will likely find that most of my writing is short, blunt and to the point. I know not everyone likes that style, but it is who I am and how I happen to look at the world. For my mind it is easier to give a single thought all my attention until I am done with that idea.

I hope you enjoy this little book and that it inspires you to search for your own truth.

-Maranda Russell

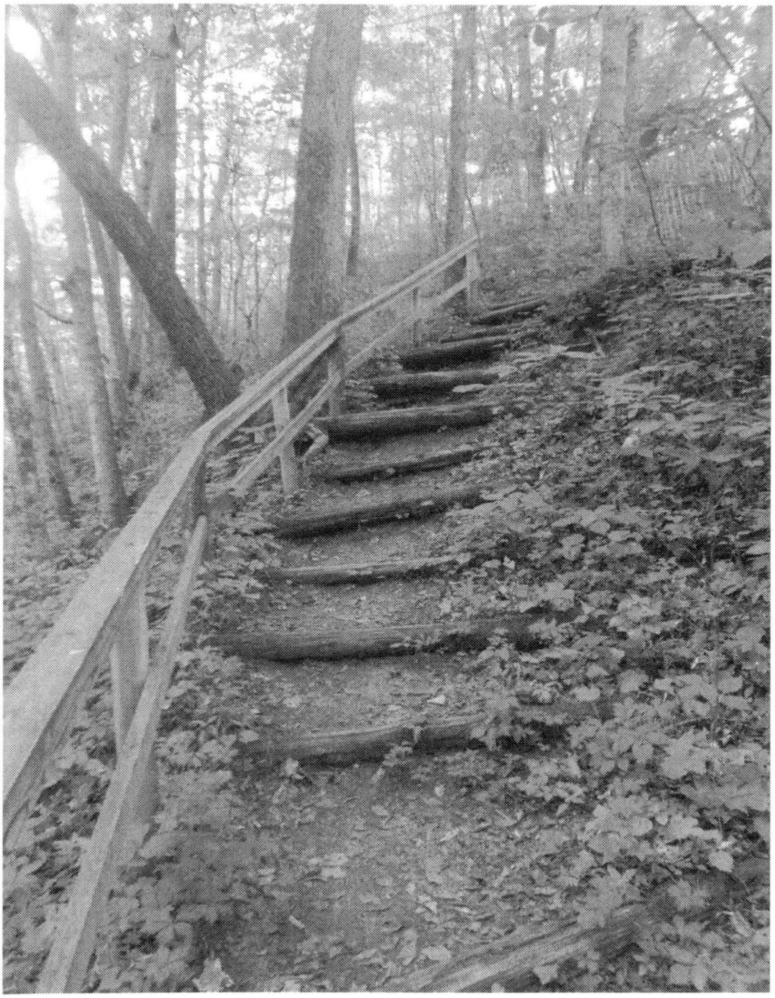

Before Your Eyes

They say
that right before you die
your life flashes before your eyes.
I don't agree.

It's more like
you suck in a breath,
unconsciously curl into a fetal
position
and pray to the universe
without words -

too stunned
to even name a God.

On the Subject of Forgiveness

I forgive you,
I truly do.
I only wish
the best for you.

However,
you are not good for me.

You choose to see
only the worst in me,
wishing me to be
too blind to see
the spark inside
which illuminates me.

Nurture the Mystery

Get comfortable with the gray areas -
get comfortable with not knowing.

Don't drain every ounce of surprise
from your existence.
Don't believe that you know it all -
and thus stop learning.

Embrace the unknown.
Embrace the confusion.
Embrace the possibilities.

And above all,
never let the mystery go -

for as the mystery goes,
so does the magic.

Long Journey Home

Sometimes it seems
like this life
is a long journey home.

But perhaps
that is because
the road rarely
lays flat,
and the promised shortcuts
serve only to lead us
back to the beginning.

Pain as a Teacher

Pain may be an effective teacher -

but it is one instructor
that will never be loved.

Life Without Art

What would life be like without art? Imagine…no music. No paintings. No literature. No movies. The list of what we would be missing just goes on and on.

Where would we turn the next time our hearts are cruelly broken?

What would give us the courage to wake up each morning and face this dull, mediocre life?

Without art, would we even know the splendor of nature? After all, isn't God the consummate artist?

The thought of life without art in its many forms is so depressing, so hopeless and so pointless that I shiver just entertaining the thought.

When was the last time you gave thanks for the art and the artists in your life?

Bitterness

You flow through my veins
like a sinister virus,

waging a war
from the inside -

until *all* has become
like you.

The Death of the Soul

The death of the soul
occurs more leisurely
than most would imagine.

A little greed here,
a little hate there -
it all adds up,
consistently pushing
your humanity downwards
until the eternal part
becomes strangled
beneath the emotional sewage.

Still, the soul is strong
and will continue to fight -

even as it decomposes.

Learning Disability

We think that we are the most evolved species on earth, but we only speak one language – human.

The rest of creation communicates effortlessly with one another in a million different languages.

When you think about it that way, you have to wonder if *we* are the ones with a learning disability.

Becoming Spiritual

I've spent so much time
trying to "become" spiritual -

not realizing
that I already was
all along.

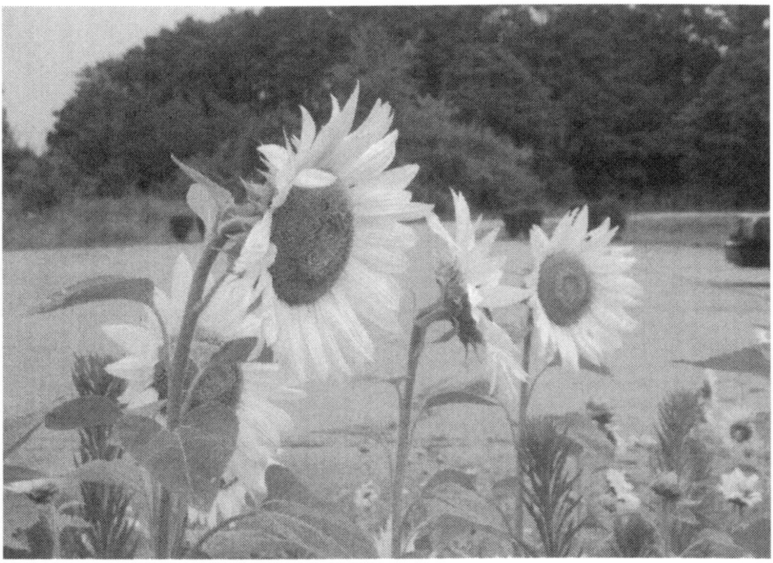

Poetry is Dead

They say poetry is dead
and maybe it is -
but so what?

Civility is dead
and apparently
so is God.

But you know what?
I always liked the dead -
lying peaceful and quiet.

So all in all,
I think I'll take my chances.

Cynical

I want to write
a happy poem
about puffy clouds
and sleepy kittens -
but when I look
to the world
for inspiration
and start to write,
my thoughts always turn
to violence,
injustice,
broken lives
and the weary, knowing eyes
of those who have seen
far too much.

After that,
clouds and kittens
just don't seem
quite as important.

But then I reconsider...
maybe puffy clouds
and sleepy kittens

are the very things we need
to help us find our way
through the pain.

Deep Thoughts at McDonald's

Sitting at McDonald's,
I am a 30-year-old woman
who just finished a happy meal -
not for the food,
but for the Barbie toy.
I guess some things never change.

Gazing out the window
beside my booth,
I watch the rain trickle down.
It strikes the black pavement
of the drive-thru,
each drop doing its own
little dance,
creating perfect little
pirouettes.

As my attention
moves to the shrubs -
silly little things
being tickled by the wind,
and the grass -
yellow, but hanging on
for dear life,

I realize

that in the end,
nature always
has its way...

and I'll always
want my toys.

Afraid

I'm afraid of dying.
I'm afraid of how it will feel.
I'm afraid of leaving this world.
I'm afraid of being forgotten.
I'm afraid of leaving those I love.

I'm afraid to meet God.
I'm afraid of judgment day.
I'm afraid of being wrong.
I'm afraid that God isn't good.
I'm afraid of not existing at all.

But most of all –

I'm afraid that my dark side
will be allowed
to create my own reality.

Life & Death

Life
is a stained
glass window
blown apart
by the winds
of a hurricane

and while the storm rages,
we know that in the end

Death
is a cold,
unforgiving secret
no one
is able
to keep.

Two Worlds

We all walk two worlds - the inner world that only we can fully see and the outer world where life flows all around us. As we walk between these two realities, our feet are sure to get tired, but we keep going anyhow.

The danger comes in when the outside world tries to dictate your inside world. Since we are all intimately connected, our inner worlds may share some similarities but they do not need to be identical. The beauty is in our own creative abilities and individual dreams.

Remember that no matter how much outside pressure you may feel to conform, in your own world you are free. After all, no prison can stop the mind from traveling where it wants or restrain the heart from believing in what it feels.

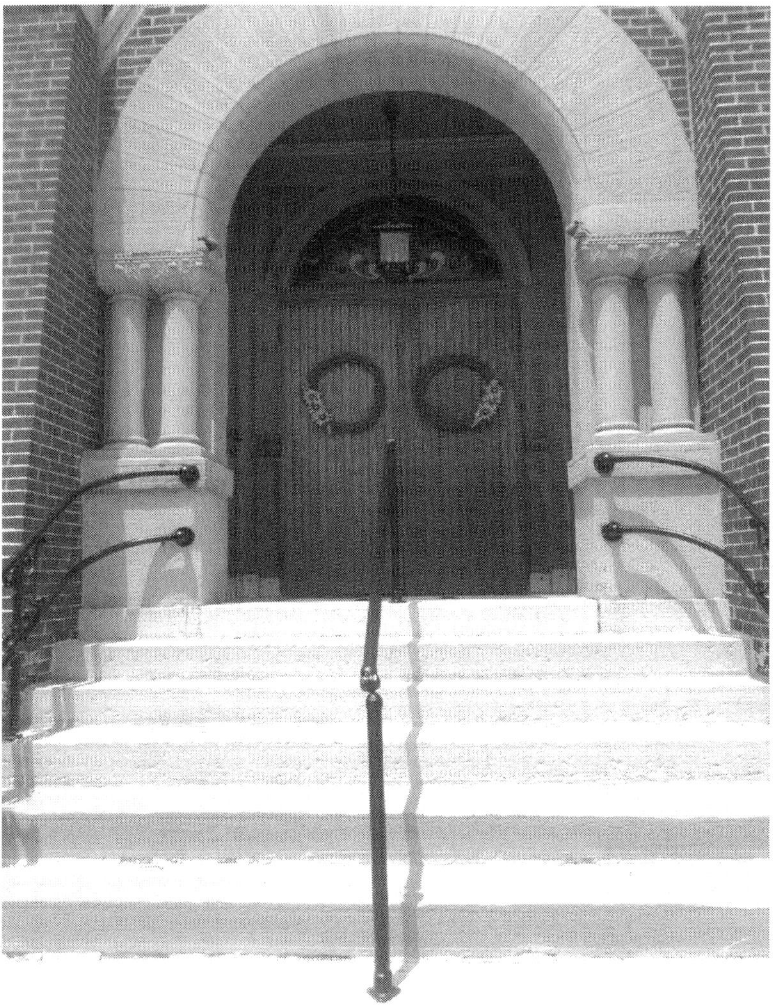

Alice in Wonderland Haiku 1 & 2

Alice in Wonderland Haiku #1

That fast white rabbit
never bothered to tell me
where the hell I am.

Alice in Wonderland Haiku #2

I'm not sure if a
caterpillar smoking blunts
will prove trustworthy.

(Side note - I include these poems because I always thought the story of *Alice in Wonderland* made for some interesting philosophical thoughts.)

On Opinions

Everyone has opinions,
but not everyone
should share theirs.

I'm sorry to tell you,
but your opinions -
no matter how closely held,
do not override
scientific fact.

Holy Books

I find it ironic
when a book
written about God
becomes more important
than the deity
who inspired it
in the first place.

Compliments

I let praise go to my head.
I sunbathe in the warm rays
of compliments
and fool myself into believing
that I'm better than
I actually am.

However, that inflated ego
keeps me going.
It makes me feel important
and like my voice counts
for something -
in a world where it normally
doesn't.

Seeking Truth

Sometimes people
cling to beliefs
from their childhood,
not because of loyalty
or heartfelt conviction -

but because they are
simply too lazy
or afraid
to search out the truth
for themselves.

Mardi Gras

If you could somehow
get inside my head
you might think you've
entered Mardi Gras.

You could be enchanted
by the whirling colors and
the glittery trinkets being
thrown through the air -
or you might be made uncomfortable
as the soul exposes itself
in words and thoughts
just to get a cheap token.

But don't worry.

We may play wanton games
for the day, but we make sure
our faces stay safely covered
by our masks
because tomorrow
always comes with a clear head.

Be Proud of Your Scars

Be proud of your scars.
Show off every dark-colored stain
that mars the perfection
of an unwritten past.

Remember every stitch,
every single thread
used to put you back together
whether you wanted it or not.

Remember the sad songs
in the middle of the night -
the ones that reopened your wounds
and allowed them to heal.

Remember those who were there,
the ones that stayed at your side
without shame or complaint.
Cherish them - for they are true friends.

Love – in Theory and Practice

Maybe I have read too many near-death experiences or just have too much time on my hands, but I often think about the end of my life and how I will feel if I undergo a life review.

While pondering, I start to wonder if the life review would make me regret some of the things I did? Or will I regret even more some of the things I could have done but didn't do? I start to wonder about what will really matter at the end. Of course, most of the time I come down to the same answer…

LOVE – the "real" purpose in life.

Not fame. Not money. Not being highly educated. Not being praised and appreciated. Not work. Not play. Not fulfilling our ego. Not collecting things. Not being the "best" at something. Not being perfect. Not wallowing in self-pity. Not being "right". Not being super-religious. Not even being "happy".

In the end, nothing but love really matters. Not the ooey-gooey, tingly feelings of budding romance, but real, true, nitty-gritty love – the kind that seeps past your bones into your very soul and gives you the will to go on when all else fails.

The hard part is that love like that is hard to find and even harder to give away on a consistent basis. To give that kind of love to others you have to overcome the all-consuming self-interest that most of us struggle with. You have to REALLY be willing to sacrifice and give yourself to others.

That kind of selfless love can be hard to give to your family, let alone to strangers. Most of us prefer to focus on the theories and philosophy of love, rather than the actual practice. It is easier and safer to stay in our heads and look logically at love, but real love can't be analyzed and figured out…it can only be given away.

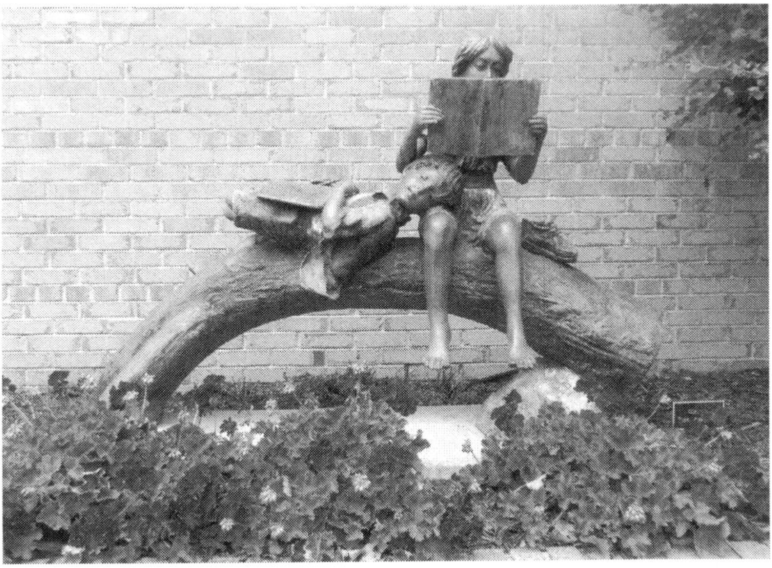

Where You Should Be

Right now
you are exactly
where you should be.
Don't allow anyone
to tell you otherwise.

Your path may have been long
and strewn with mistakes
but that is life.
We all make wrong turns
and false starts.
Sometimes we even
give up.

We cry,
we scream,
we rail at the world -
and we pout...

but eventually,
we move on.

At that point,
we pick ourselves up,

dust ourselves off
and get back
to our purpose.

Religion is a Box

Religion is a box -
a tight, often stifling box.

A box I once spent far
too long trapped inside.
A box with chains and
manacles.

A box that punishes
movement -
even an innocent attempt
to peer over the edge.

When I left the box,
it wasn't easy or
painless.
My skin was ripped away,
leaving raw wounds
as I broke free from
the constraints.

To this day,
bits of my flesh
and blood still lay

entwined with metal,
resting silently
within that cage's
battered walls.

Labels

The labels we give ourselves -
Democrat, Republican,
conservative, liberal -
why do we let these
names
fool us
into believing
that's all we are?

The truth is
we need each other
like it
or not.

Left to ourselves
and those of our kind,
we lose balance
and perspective.

We forget

that there's a whole world
outside
of our own narrow view.

A world of trouble,
a world of tragedy.
A world that
desperately
needs our help.

A world
that doesn't benefit at all
from another pointless debate.

Fighting Fear

Fear stops me
from doing so many things.
I let it psyche me out
to the point
that I never do anything -
not even those things
I most long to try.

I tell myself to rise above -
to suck it up
and jump on in,
even if I have to
close my eyes
and hold my breath
to make it through.

Yet no matter
how many promises I make myself
or how many times I say I'll be stronger,
the fear always seems
to come out the victor -

leaving me feeling frustrated, cowardly
and completely unfulfilled.

Creative License

What do you do
when someone
revokes
your creative license?

Do you give up the keys
and get out of the car -

or do you press the pedal
all the way
to the floor

and escape
as soon as you can?

I Was Made This Way for a Reason

I was made this way
for a reason...

With a mind that chases down ideas
and wrestles them to the ground.

With eyes that pierce the veil
then hide themselves from the darkness.

With ears that hear you say one thing
but intuit something else altogether.

With a mouth that may seem too bold
but seeks only to speak the truth.

With a heart that casts out a net
to catch every casualty floating by.

With arms wishing to embrace the cosmos
but returning empty, feeling bereft.

With feet that stumble over themselves,
yet constantly rise and keep going.

Yes,
I was made this way
for a reason...

and so were you.

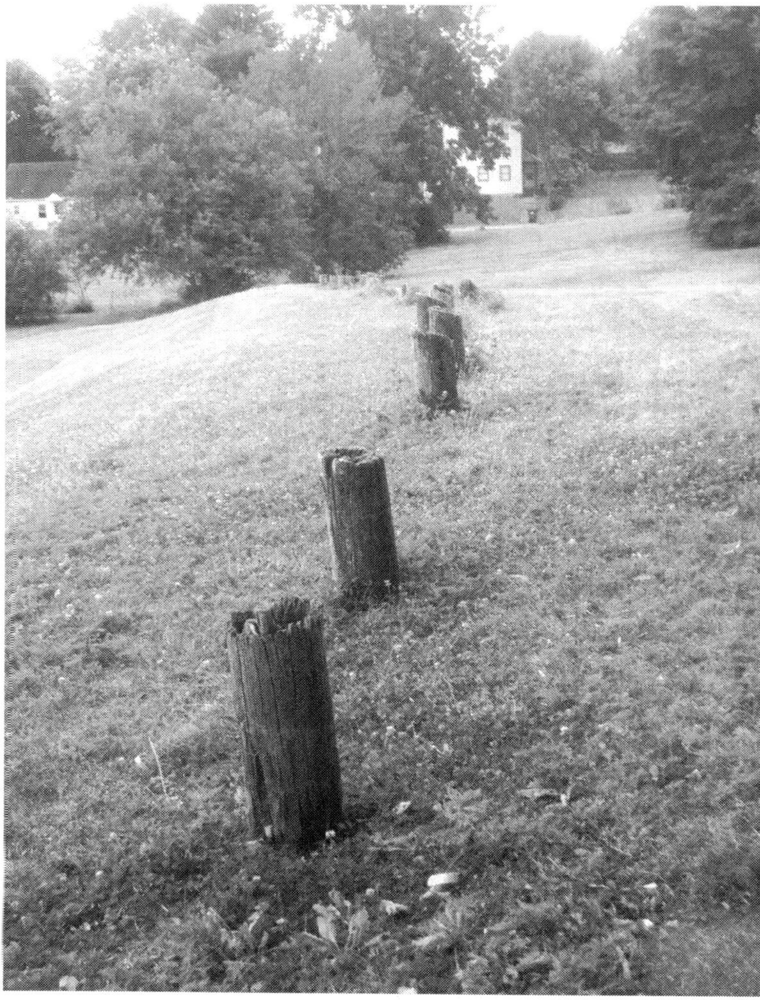

Love in Theory

It's funny how people
can sit around
and talk about love -
yet show none
to those around them.

They debate about
love's meaning -
is love conditional?
is love blind?
is love truly
meant for all?

Maybe,
just maybe,
if they shut their mouths
and opened their eyes,

love
could finally
make an appearance.

Angels and Fairies

Walking through the art museum gift shop,
I spy a pair of blue wings.

Turning to you, I ask,
"Did you know that legend says
fairies are just fallen angels
who weren't bad enough
to fall all the way to hell?"

"Maybe we're the fairies," you reply.

"Where are our wings?" I ask
as I try on a smooth copper bracelet.

"We lost them when we fell."

I consider and nod my head.
"At least we got a second chance."

You pull out your Visa and hand it to me.
As we walk to the register,
I'm suddenly hit with a sharp
yearning.

"I hope I get my wings back when I die!"

"Don't worry," you console.
"I promise I'll ring a bell for you."

True Psychic Powers

Once,
I tried to make a living
as a psychic -
just to see
if I actually could.

The people came to me -
their fists full
of personal angst,
and their heads sloshing over
with tough questions
about jobs,
failed love affairs
and the most recent family drama.

But you know what I found?

It wasn't paranormal wisdom
or sleight of hand
they were looking for.
No tea leaves or tarot cards,
no astrological charts.

Instead,

what they really wanted
was a little bit of common sense
and to know without a doubt
that someone -
ANYONE
cared enough to listen.

Mildew

Doubt is its own
kind of mildew.
You scrub and scrub
to make it leave,

only to turn your back -
and have it take up
residence
once again.

Jerks and Idiots

I find it hard
to forgive jerks
and idiots,
but I forgive them anyhow.

Why?

Because looking back,
I recall times
others forgave me
for the exact same reason.

The Secret to Life

Buddha once told us
the secret to life -

Never fear
what will become of you
and depend on no one.
Furthermore,
reject all help
and then find freedom.

I know the Buddha was wise
and revered -
but honestly,
his secret to life
sounds terribly sad
and lonely to me.

(Side note – I generally like Buddha and his teachings, I just found this teaching rather cold and sad.)

Time and Circumstance

My hope
is set on heaven,
but my fears
are set on doubt.

Afraid that time
and circumstance
may wash
the whole thing out.

Schrodinger's Cat

Just like with
Schrodinger's cat,
I find that
it *is* possible
to be both
dead
and alive
at the same time.

About the Author

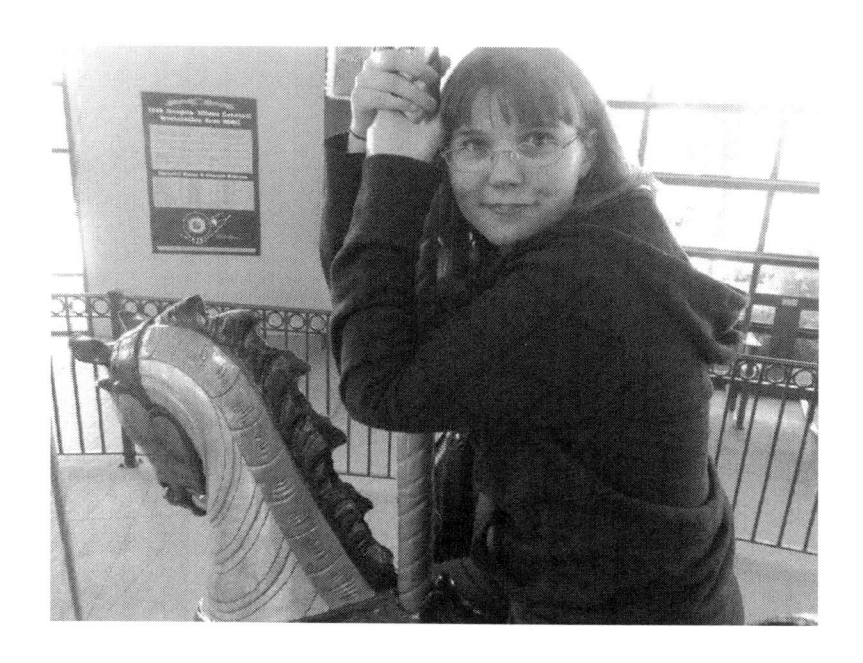

Maranda Russell is an artist, author, poet and cat lover who also happens to have Asperger's Syndrome (a kind of high-functioning autism). She currently lives in Dayton, Ohio with her husband and six cats.

If you have a comment or question for Maranda, please visit her website, www.marandarussell.com, email her at Shojobeatgirl@live.com or find her on Facebook!

If you enjoyed this book or have comments to share, please consider leaving a review on Amazon!

Made in the USA
Lexington, KY
22 April 2019